REAL LIVES

Tudor Children

Four True Life Stories

SALLIE PURKIS

Contents

A & C Black • London

Living in Tudor Times

C an you imagine growing up in Tudor times, like the four children in this book? Your life would have been very different from life today.

In Tudor times, nearly every new baby was christened in church soon after birth. The name and birth date of every new-born baby had to be written in the church register by law. A christening was a time to celebrate that a baby was alive, as many died soon after they were born. Many mothers in Tudor times also died in childbirth. Most mothers breast fed their babies, but those who could afford to paid for their baby to be looked after by a 'wet nurse'. She was a mother with a baby of her own, who could also breast feed another baby.

Parents tried very hard to keep their children away from infections. There were no injections or medicines to

protect babies as there are today. Deadly diseases such as smallpox and the plague spread quickly, particularly in towns, where lots of people lived close together so germs spread more easily. There was very little clean water and no proper drains. David, one of the children in this book, was unusual because he survived an attack of smallpox.

Most families lived in the country and had a piece of land where they could grow vegetables and keep a few chickens or a cow. They could use what they grew to feed the family or to sell at the market. Women made butter and cheese for their families and sold any surplus at the local market. They made their own bread, and smoked ham, bacon and fish over the fire to preserve it for winter, as there were no fridges or freezers. Meat was a luxury. Fish was much cheaper.

Ordinary families made their own clothes, spinning sheep's wool into yarn and then weaving it into a piece of cloth. They also made jackets and bed coverings from sheepskin. Merchants imported velvet and silk from India or China, but only the very rich could afford to buy them. Rich people had their clothes made for them.

Everyone had to go to church on Sunday. As well as saying prayers and listening to Bible readings, people were told important news by the priest, as there were no televisions or radios at that time. The priest was also supposed to teach the local children to count and to read the Lord's Prayer. Rich families employed a tutor to teach their children at home, but many new schools for boys were also opened in towns like Chester, where Thomas went to school. Here, boys were taught Latin, Greek and geometry as well as English. All children were taught to behave well and to have good manners.

In this book, you can read short biographies of four children who lived in Tudor times. We have collected information about the children from fragments of historical evidence (see pages 4 and 5). No pictures of them have survived and only David left behind some writing about his own life. Although they lived in different places and had very different experiences, they were all alive in 1588 when the Spanish Armada was defeated. They would all have seen the beacons lit across the country to warn people of the arrival of the Spanish fleet and they would all have taken part in the victory celebrations.

Thomas lived here with his family. His father was rich and important and became Mayor of Chester.

Em lived here with her family. They all worked on the farm that was attached to their family house.

David was born here and lived here until he went to boarding school in London when he was 12.

Catherine was born here in her parents' mansion. King Henry VIII's sixth wife was her godmother.

How we know

A biography is the story of someone's life written by another person. A biographer can use many different sources of information to write the story. It is quite hard to find information about Tudor children, but these are some of the sources we have used to find out about the lives of the four children in this book.

Autobiographies

An autobiography is the story someone writes about their own life. When David was an adult in Rome he wrote down memories of his childhood, and a copy of his book is kept among the documents of his old school.

Church memorials

Memorials, tombs and brasses inside churches tell us about important Tudor people who once worshipped there. Thomas Gamull, who you will read about in this book, has his tomb in St Mary's Heritage Centre in Chester.

Wills and inventories

People in Tudor times sometimes left a written will saying to whom they wanted to leave their belongings when they died. Looking at wills can tell us something about people's lives. Another way of finding out about the past is to look at inventories. After a death, friends and relatives went through the person's house, writing down all their possessions in a list called an inventory. We found out about Em's farm from an inventory.

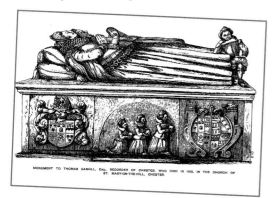

MONUMENT TO THOMAS GAMULL, Esq., RECORDER OF CHESTER, WHO DIED IN 1613, IN THE CHURCH OF ST. MARY-ON-THE-HILL, CHESTER.

Houses

Some homes built in Tudor times are still lived in today, although they have been modernized and made more comfortable inside, for example having running water installed. Several large country houses, like Catherine's home, Ingatestone Hall, are open to the public.

Maps

Tudor map-makers were famous. They travelled all over the country drawing maps of towns, villages, rivers and other natural features. With these maps we can see what towns were like in Tudor times. This one shows Chester, where Thomas lived.

Pictures of people

Wealthy families often had their portrait painted by a fashionable artist, to hang in their homes. Pictures to illustrate books were carved onto a wooden block, which could be used to print the picture. These books were about subjects such as farming and fishing, or were story books. Many show ordinary Tudor people at work.

The Cottage Housewife

Parish registers

From 1538, priests were instructed to keep records of all the births, marriages and burials in their parish. A few of these ancient records have survived and are kept in County Record Offices.

Household accounts

Big houses, such as Ingatestone Hall, where Catherine lived, kept careful accounts of the money they spent. These included the expenses of having people, such as Queen Elizabeth I, to stay. The cost of the food, the entertainment and extra payments made to servants were all listed.

CATHERINE

C atherine was born in 1544 during King Henry VIII's reign. She lived in Ingatestone Hall, a country house in Essex. This new red-brick house had large windows and beautiful chimneys.

Sir William Petre was the King's Secretary and he travelled around England on royal business. Shortly before Catherine was born, he was made a special adviser to the king's sixth wife, Catherine Parr. The queen agreed to be a godmother to the new baby, who was immediately named Catherine! There was a big christening party for Catherine, at which the guests drank French wine, ate cakes and gave presents to the baby.

Soon afterwards, she was taken away to one of the farms owned by her parents to be looked after and fed by a wet nurse, the farmer's wife. She would have stayed there for about a year. This was normal for babies of wealthy families in Tudor times.

Catherine's father began building this house four years before she was born. The family still live in the house which is also open to the public.

Both Sir William and Lady Anne had been married before and had other children. Catherine had three half-sisters, as well as an older sister and a younger brother. The family all lived together at Ingatestone, and sometimes went for short visits to their other house in London.

Ingatestone was never empty. As well as the children, there were 21 indoor servants who all wore a special grey uniform called a livery. One servant, Mistress Mary, was in charge of the children. She taught Catherine to sing and to have good manners, to say her prayers, to learn psalms from the Bible by heart, and to read. A music teacher came regularly to teach the girls to play the virginals, which was a musical instrument a bit like a piano. They also learned to ride a horse.

At mealtimes Mistress Mary ate with the family in the dining room, and at night she slept with Catherine and her sisters in the bedroom they all shared. The other servants ate in the Servant's Hall, which was a huge room just inside the front door.

There were lots of visitors to Ingatestone and it was the custom in Tudor times to provide them with food, drink and a place to sleep, even if you did not know them or expect them. There was always plenty of extra food for any visitors who happened to call. Sir William had to travel a lot, but when he was at home, messengers came on horseback to deliver notes from the king as there was no postal service.

Craftsmen, such as tilers, blacksmiths, wheelwrights and glaziers, who travelled around the country, often called at the house to work on parts of the building. Tailors and

We can find out a lot about life at Ingatestone from the household accounts, which have survived from Catherine's time.

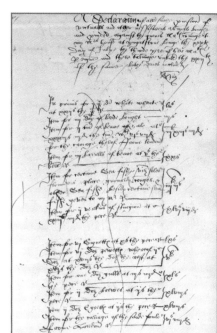

dressmakers came to measure the family for any clothes they needed for a special occasion. When important guests from Court or other great houses visited, they would bring their own servants with them.

Many of the household accounts from the time when Catherine was growing up have survived. They show that the names of the guests were always written down, along with the food they ate and how much it all cost.

Much of the food Catherine ate was grown on the family farm. Servants ground wheat and rye into flour, which the cook made into different sorts of bread at the bakehouse. Catherine and her sister liked going there to watch the dough rise. They also visited the dairy where butter and cheese were made; they collected hen's eggs and watched the pigs, cows and sheep. They ate roast meat when one of the animals was killed, and at other times they ate fish and wild ducks from local ponds. The cook often made pies from pigeons, partridges, pheasants and rabbits from their woods, caught by the gamekeeper.

Catherine ate fruit from the orchard and green vegetables from the garden. Herbs from the garden added flavour to the food and they were also used to make medicine. There was very little clean drinking water and even children drank the light ale that was made in the brewhouse.

Christmas time was always special and Catherine loved it. The holiday lasted for 12 days and Sir William hurried from court to spend time at home. Acrobats, actors and musicians arrived at the house to entertain everyone, and there were special treats, such as dried fruit from Spain and spiced biscuits.

Several members of the royal family visited Ingatestone and Catherine met them all. Princess Mary, King Henry's eldest daughter, had a house only two hour's ride away. She first visited when Catherine was three and she stayed for two nights. The princess must have enjoyed her visit because the next week she came again, and when Catherine's brother John was born she made a third visit to see the new baby.

When Catherine was eight, Mary became queen. On her way to be crowned in London, Mary stopped at Ingatestone. Catherine and her sister helped their mother welcome all the important people who gathered to greet Mary, and after supper they helped organise the entertainment. They may have played the virginals or joined in the singing and dancing.

The most memorable visitor of all was Queen Elizabeth I, who announced that she would spend three days and nights at Ingatestone in July 1561. Catherine was very excited, and the household went into a spin making preparations. New curtains and furnishings had to be made for the royal bedroom, fine silver plates and jugs for the table, and extra

food and wine were stored in the cellars. Outside, bricklayers and carpenters even built extra buildings to house all the queen's servants and horses.

When the day arrived, the queen and her procession turned into the long drive leading to Ingatestone at around noon. The queen was in a leather coach decorated with feathers. Catherine and her family, along with their servants, lined up outside the front entrance to greet her. Three days of magnificent feasts and entertainment followed.

WHEN CATHERINE GREW UP

One month after Queen Elizabeth's visit there was another celebration. Catherine, aged 16, was married. Catherine's husband came from Worcestershire, but she seems to have spent a lot of time at Ingatestone. She had three children who were all born there, and she and her family continued to spend time at the house.

EM

E m Bateman was born during Queen Mary I's reign, in a tiny village high in the Cotswold hills in Gloucestershire. Both her parents were farmers and Em spent all her life working on the farm.

We do not know Em's full first name or exactly when she was born, but it was probably around 1555, about three years before Elizabeth became queen. We know a little about the family from the will Em's father wrote. He left his belongings to Em, her sister and their brother. There is also a list, called an inventory, of everything in his house and farmyard. From this we can work out what the farm was like and how Em and her family lived.

Baby Em slept in a wooden cradle that her father, Thomas, had made. When she was about six months old, her parents began to feed her a porridge mixture called pap, which was made from bits of bread soaked in milk. They were pleased to see her thrive, as many babies died soon after they were born. This was because disease spread easily but only rich people could afford doctors.

We know about Em and her family from her father's will, which can be seen today in the Record Office in Gloucester.

12

The Batemans, like everyone else in the village, went to church every Sunday, and baby Em would have been christened there. The church still stands today. As Em grew older, she learned to join in with prayers such as the Lord's Prayer from the new English prayer book, and she listened to the priest reading from the English Bible. Em may have gone to reading and writing lessons given by the priest, but most of what she knew she learned from her mother.

Em's father owned some land and also had the right to grow corn and vegetables on strips of land in the village fields. His farm was in a fertile area and, if the whole family worked hard, they could grow enough food for themselves. They also had sheep, and some years they were able to sell fleeces that they did not need for their own clothes and bedding to a merchant in the nearby big town of Northleach.

St. Andrews church in Hazleton, where Em was christened.

Thomas built his own house using local materials. He used wood to build the frame and limestone from a quarry near the village for the walls. The spaces were filled with small branches and twigs, and the whole lot was cemented in with a mixture of powdered limestone, clay and animal dung. This mixture was called wattle and daub. The house had a thatched roof.

Inside, it was rather like a big barn, with an upstairs floor that was reached by a ladder. The family slept up here on sheep fleeces. There was no glass for the windows. Wooden shutters kept out the cold, but made it very dark inside when they were closed.

Downstairs there was a fireplace where Em's mother kept the fire burning day and night. It kept the whole family warm and gave some light when the shutters were closed. Em helped her mother carry in wood for the fire from a very young age and watched her pile it on an iron stand called a trestle. There was no bathroom in Em's house. The family washed in a bowl of water, and the toilet (called a privy) was just an earth pit in the farmyard.

Em got up at sunrise with the rest of her family, to feed the animals. The cow had to be milked and the eggs collected from the hens. Em, her mother and sister made butter and cheese from any milk that was not needed that day. Next, they ground some of their corn into flour and made bread.

Sometimes they took the sheep to graze on the common, which was a large area of grass used by everyone in the village. Em and her sister would watch the sheep to make sure they did not wander away or get taken home by someone else. From the surrounding fields and hedgerows Em helped her mother and sister collect thistles for the pigs to eat, rushes to put on the floor and, in summer, sweet-smelling flowers to make the house smell fresh. Sometimes they rode seven miles on horseback to Northleach market to sell any spare produce, such as eggs or butter, or to buy things they could not grow themselves, such as salt and spices.

Em loved the delicious stews her mother made in a big iron pot, which swung from a hook above the fire. Normally the stews were made of vegetables, but some days they included a rabbit or some other meat. One treat that Em looked forward to was a family meal of a whole chicken or big piece of meat, when one of their animals was killed. It was skewered on an iron spit in front of the fire, where it was turned round and round until it was cooked on all sides.

After dark the only lighting in the house was from a rush dipped in fat. The family also stoked up the fire.

While the meat was cooking, Em's mother collected the fat in a pan as it dripped off the turning meat. She used it to

make candles or rush lights. She would dip the rushes into the fat and then place them in a holder on the wall. The fat-dipped rushes burned slowly, giving off some light, but also lots of smoke and a bad smell.

Em usually ate her food from a homemade wooden plate and drank out of cups made from the horns of cows, but her family was rich enough to have some pewter plates and dishes too, which were used on special occasions.

Em's favourite time of year was the summer, even though there was hay making to do and the harvest to bring in. As soon as her father and brother sheared the sheep, she was shown how to wash and comb the wool. She was proud of the way she could spin the clean wool into a thread and then weave it into cloth for clothes and blankets. When a sheep was killed, the fleece was used on the beds to keep the family warm in winter, or made into a sleeveless jacket.

When it grew dark, the whole family went up the ladder to bed. They had three beds and Em had to share with her sister Joan. Em had to be ready to start another busy day as soon as it was light enough to see.

WHEN EM GREW UP
There are no records to show that Em ever left Hazelton or that she got married. We know from her father's will that she was still living on the farm in 1587 when she was about 33.

THOMAS

T homas was born in Chester in 1571. His father was an important businessman. Thomas received a good education at a grammar school and later went to Oxford University.

Chester is on the River Dee, and in Tudor times it was the most important and prosperous port in the northwest of England. Many wealthy merchants lived there. They made money from selling local goods to other places all over Europe, as well as buying foreign goods to sell in England. The goods came and went in ships that sailed up and down the Dee. Thomas's father, Edmund Gamull, was a wealthy merchant and businessman, and his mother, Elizabeth, was also rich as she had inherited property from her first husband. Thomas was their first child.

This map of Chester was drawn when Thomas was alive and shows the streets and buildings he saw every day.

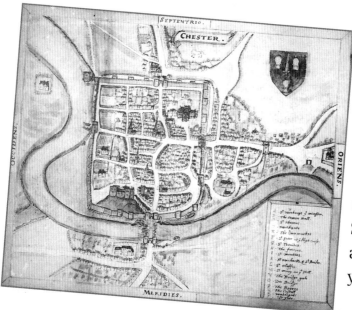

Thomas was christened in St Mary's Church. His parents employed a wet nurse to look after him. She was someone who had just had a baby of her own and could provide milk for Thomas as well as her own baby. She would have looked after Thomas for about a year, until he could drink cow's milk from a cup. Thomas thrived as a baby, unlike his younger brother, John, who died only a few days after he was born. Families became used to death in Tudor times. There were few doctors and there were lots of germs because it was difficult to keep everything clean. Thomas's mother went on to have three girls and one more boy in the next five years, but soon after her last daughter was born, she died. Two years later, when Thomas was ten, his father married again. Thomas's stepmother was also called Elizabeth, as his mother had been.

Chester was an exciting place to live. From his bedroom, Thomas could hear the mills on the River Dee clanking and grinding away, the sailors and fishermen calling down the river and the market traders taking live animals to market in the centre of town.

Mills were built on the riverbank and had large water wheels that were turned by the flow of the river. Thomas's father had six for grinding corn and two for raising water into the town. The other three were fulling mills used to make woollen cloth.

Some days Edmund would take Thomas and his brother to High Cross, to show them where the merchants met to discuss which ships were in, which were expected and what they would be carrying. They visited the nearby Wool Hall where raw wool and cloth were sold, or the bustling cornmarket where grain was traded. They often went inside the beautiful cathedral, which had been an abbey before it was closed down by King Henry VIII.

From home, Thomas could walk round the town walls or play in the ruins of the old Norman castle. Sometimes Thomas and his brothers and sisters were taken to climb the water tower, which overlooked the harbour, and from where they could watch the ships coming and going.

The family owned the house they lived in and they also owned 11 mills nearby and other land in town. The town house where Thomas lived was three storeys high. On the lowest floor, which was mostly underground, were cellars and warehouses where Edmund stored wine and other goods that he imported. On the next floor was the great hall, which was the centre of activity. There was little privacy, as the family and their many servants all ate their meals and spent most of their time there. The house was designed with a ramp, called a row, that went directly into the upper floor, and the great hall could be reached by a stairway from the street outside.

On the top floor there were bedrooms and sitting rooms for the family. At the back of the house there was a herb garden and an orchard.

Some of the Tudor houses in Chester have survived, but not the one where Thomas lived.

Thomas was probably taught to read the alphabet and the Lord's Prayer at home, but in September 1579, when he was eight years old, he went to the King's School in Chester. This had been founded by King Henry VIII nearly 40 years before. Thomas stayed at the King's School for four years. The boys all sat in one big schoolroom and were taught to write using a quill pen made from a goose feather. Thomas had to study Latin, Greek, arithmetic and geometry.

Thomas was taught to have good manners and was expected to be obedient. If he did not listen to his teacher, or if he behaved badly, he was beaten with a bundle of birch twigs.

When Thomas was 14, his father was elected Mayor of Chester. Thomas was excited to see his father dressed in official robes, leading the procession of aldermen and councillors into the Common Hall, where their meetings were held. Thomas watched him carrying the great sword of Chester, which is shown on the city's coat of arms. Little did Thomas know that one day he would also hold an important position in Chester.

Chester was an enjoyable place to be on public holidays and special occasions. Everyone in town looked forward to the Midsummer Fair, which lasted for three days in June.

There were stalls with refreshments, and Thomas particularly enjoyed the entertainment, which included musicians, storytellers, acrobats and jugglers. Some actors even dressed up as giants!

Whitsun, the seventh Sunday after Easter, was another special occasion. Ordinary workers from the town set up carts in the square in front of the cathedral to make a stage. Each group performed a play based on a story from the Bible. These were called Mystery Plays. The performers moved the carts around the town, stopping at various places to stage the plays. The townspeople flocked to watch them.

Thomas's family also owned a country house, called Crabwell Hall, in Mollington, which was about two miles outside Chester. In the summer, when the town became hot and smelly, and when there was a chance of catching the plague, Thomas and his family escaped to the house for some country air.

Thomas's tomb in St Mary's Heritage Centre in Chester. Thomas's wife, Alice, found an artist to carve his portrait on the tomb. It also shows their three dead babies and a statue of their son, Francis, who survived.

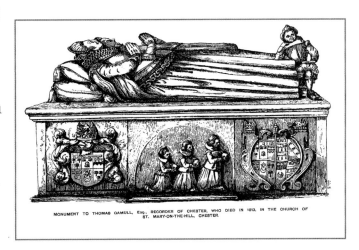

MONUMENT TO THOMAS GAMULL, Esq., RECORDER OF CHESTER, WHO DIED IN 1613, IN THE CHURCH OF ST. MARY-ON-THE-HILL, CHESTER.

WHEN THOMAS GREW UP

When he was 16, Thomas went to Oxford University and later became a lawyer. He also became the Chester City Recorder, an important position. He married Alice and had four children, but three of them died soon after birth. Thomas died aged 42.

DAVID

David was born in December 1575, in Abergavenny, a market town in the foothills of the Black Mountains in Wales. He was the youngest of 13 children and his father was the Sheriff of Monmouth.

Soon after David was born, he was taken about five miles outside the town to live with a wet nurse in the countryside. He thrived on the good milk and fresh air and only returned to live with his own family when he was old enough to eat adult food.

Most of what we know about David comes from the autobiography he wrote as an adult, although we don't know if everything he wrote is true. In it, he tells lots of stories

about his childhood. We know that when he was three, he caught smallpox, which was a very infectious disease a little like chickenpox. David was lucky to survive, as most people died from smallpox.

When David was seven years old, he almost drowned. He was hanging over a bridge, watching his sisters float paper boats down the stream. He leaned out further for a better view and fell into the fast-flowing river. Luckily, a man who had just passed over the bridge heard the cries of people on the bank and jumped into the water to save David's life.

David was well known in Abergavenny because he had a beautiful singing voice. From the age of four, he had singing lessons and learned to sing church anthems and prayers. He was soon good enough to join the choir. Most people in Abergavenny spoke Welsh, and David probably learned to speak Welsh from his wet nurse. However, at home he spoke in English. At school, he had to learn to read and speak in English and Latin.

When David was 12 years old, there was a big change in his life. His uncle, who was a famous lawyer, arranged for him to go to a school in London. David set off from home straight after Christmas in 1586 and he travelled for more than five weeks. He rode on horseback or in a carriage that bumped along the rough roads, and sometimes on a boat along a river. The weather was often very bad and it was a long and difficult journey, especially for a child.

We have no details of where David stayed on the way, but we do know that he arrived, tired and dirty, at Christ's Hospital School in the City of London on 8 February, 1587. On that day, the church bells were ringing to announce the execution of Mary Queen of Scots.

The schoolmaster and his wife were there to welcome David and they gave him his school uniform. All the boys wore a white shirt with a white scarf, long yellow stockings, breeches that buttoned just below the knee, a long navy blue coat and a flat hat. When people saw the boys in the street they gave them the nickname 'blue coat' boys. There were no girls at the school.

The boys slept in dormitories and at meal times they sat at long tables, just like a big family. Every morning, they took it in turns to read from the Bible, and every evening they read prayers from the new prayer book.

In the big schoolroom, they had lessons in English, Latin and Greek grammar. They learned to write in the latest handwriting style, and they also learned philosophy, talking about different people's ideas about the world.

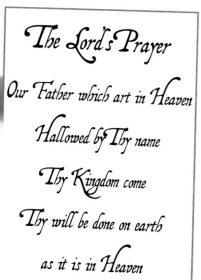

The Lord's Prayer

Our Father which art in Heaven

Hallowed by Thy name

Thy Kingdom come

Thy will be done on earth

as it is in Heaven

David used a quill pen made from a feather to write in this italic style.

On Sundays, the boys went to church in a procession. Here, they listened to the priest's sermon and also heard the latest news about national and international events.

London was an exciting place to be for David. Queen Elizabeth and her royal court were there for most of the year, and ships from all over the world came into the port of London. They

Rich people liked fine textiles, such as these highly embroidered gloves c.1595.

brought items David had never seen before, such as beautiful textiles, fine glass, spices and French and German wines. London merchants bought these and sold wool, salt and grain from Britain in return. The merchants would meet in the street near the school each day to exchange news about trading opportunities or to change foreign money they had earned abroad.

Sometimes David and his fellow pupils were asked to join in processions organised by the Lord Mayor of London. These were wonderful occasions when the streets were lined with

decorative arches, and actors, musicians and jugglers entertained the waiting crowds. David walked with his school friends in front of the main coach, where the mayor sat in all his finery with his gold chain round his neck.

Part of the Grey Friars Monastry, or Christs Hospital London.

David was at school in 1588 when there were great celebrations throughout London. There were bonfires everywhere and dancing in the streets when news came that a fleet of warships called the Spanish Armada, sent to attack Briain, had been defeated after a sea battle which lasted six days. More than a thousand Spanish soldiers on board had been killed.

This old engraving shows part of Christ's Hospital where David went to school. The school was in an old monastery building.

Two years later, at the age of 15, David was old enough to leave school and go to Oxford University.

WHEN DAVID GREW UP
David became a Catholic priest and went to live in Rome, Italy. It was illegal to be a Catholic in Britain during Queen Elizabeth I's reign. Three hundred years later, Christ's Hospital moved from London to new school buildings in Sussex. There are now girls at the school but the pupils still wear the same Tudor uniform that David wore.

Time line

National events		Personal events

National events	Year	Personal events
	1544	**Catherine** born and named after Queen Catherine Parr, Henry VIII's sixth wife.
Edward VI becomes king.	**1547**	
First English prayer book introduced.	**1549**	**Catherine's** brother John born.
Christ's Hospital founded. Mary becomes queen. England a Catholic country again.	**1553**	
	1555	**Em** born in Hazleton, Gloucestershire.
Elizabeth becomes queen.	**1558**	
	1561	Queen Elizabeth visits Ingatestone for the first time.
	1571	**Thomas** born in Chester.
	1575	**David** born in Abergavenny.
First theatre built in London.	**1576**	
	1577	**Thomas's** mother dies.
	1579	**Thomas** enters King's School, Chester.
Francis Drake returns after first British circumnavigation of the globe.	**1580**	
	1581	Thomas's father marries again.
	1583	**Thomas** leaves King's School.
First group of British families arrived to settle in Roanoke on the east coast of America. The expedition was organised by Walter Raleigh.	**1585**	**Thomas's** father becomes Mayor of Chester.
	1586	**David** travels to school in London.
Execution of Mary Queen of Scots.	**1587**	
Defeat of Spanish Armada celebrated throughout the land.	**1588**	
	1590	**David** goes to Oxford University.
Death of Queen Elizabeth.	**1603**	

30

How to find out more

Visit a Tudor house

Some Tudor houses are open to the public. You can find out if there are any in your area from your Tourist Information Office, library, the National Trust handbook or by looking at their website at www.nationaltrust.org.uk. Some of the larger houses have portraits of people who lived there in Tudor times. Many timber-framed houses like the one Em's father built for his family have also survived in some parts of the country.

Visit a farming museum

Farming methods did not really change until the invention of steam power in Queen Victoria's time. Look at a display of hand tools and pictures of how they were used. This will tell you about the work Em and her family used to do.

Visit a country church

Most village churches were built before the 16th century. Some people left money to the church for a memorial or chapel, where people could pray for them.

Take part in living history

Some museums or houses, such as Kentwell Hall in Suffolk, arrange events at which visitors pretend to be Tudor people. Ask for details from your Tourist Information Office or local museum.

Log on and surf

<www.wealddown.co.uk>

You can see old buildings rebuilt in this open-air museum to preserve them for posterity. The market place and Bayleaf farmstead will give you an idea about Em's life, and the watermill is like those owned by Thomas's father in Chester.

<www.kentwell.co.uk>

Look for pictures of the people who go to Kentwell Hall to live like Tudors for two weeks in the summer.

<www.chestercc.gov.uk/heritage>

Follow the link to the Heritage Centre in St Mary's Church where Thomas Gamull's tomb is. You can see many of the buildings from Thomas's time on the Millennium Festival Trail.

<www.christs-hospital.org.uk>

See photographs of the pupils today, who still wear the same uniform as David did.

Things to do

Write a diary

Choose one of the children in the book and write about a day in their life, e.g. David's arrival in London after his long journey; Thomas's first day at school; the day Princess Mary visited the family at Ingatestone; Em's day at the market.

Imagine a conversation

Compare the experiences of two of the children in the book. First list anything that was the same about them, then list what was different. Imagine a conversation they might have had if they had met.

Become a tourist guide

Find a picture of a Tudor house in a book or on the Internet. Write a few paragraphs to encourage tourists to visit it, or details of what you would tell a party of visitors about life there in Tudor times.

Research Tudor clothes

Imagine you have been invited to go to a living history event like those held at Kentwell (see the website). Choose a person you would like to be or a job you would like to do. Find out what kind of clothes they would have worn and what they would do at the event.

Reading list

The books listed below give an insight into life in Tudor times. Look them up in your library.

A document pack for schools called *Thomas Bateman, Tudor Farmer* is available from the Gloucestershire Record Office, Clarence Row, Alvin Street, Gloucester GL2 3DW.
Janet Axworthy, *Tudor Chester: A Resource Pack* is available from Chester Education, Grosvenor Museum, 27 Grosvenor Street, Chester, CH1 2DD.
Tony Kelly, *Children in Tudor England*, Stanley Thornes.
Sallie Purkis, *Your Tudor Locality*, Longman.
Sallie Purkis, *Tudor Life*, Longman.
Laura Wilson, *Daily Life in a Tudor House*, Heinemann.
Alison Uttley, *A Traveller in Time*, Penguin.
Elizabeth Newbery, *Tudor Farmhouse – What happened here?* A & C Black.

Places to visit

Ingatestone Hall, Hall Lane, Ingatestone, Essex
CM49 NR (01277 353010)
Catherine's old home is still owned by her family
and is open to the public in the summer months.

St Mary's Church Centre, Chester (01244 402110)
You can see Thomas's tomb here with a statue of
him as he was when he died in1613.

The Museum of London
(www.museum-london.org.uk)
Tudor and Early Stuart Galleries
Some of the things used in London when David was
at school are on display.

Speke Hall, Liverpool
(www.spekehall@nationaltrust.org.uk)
This is a house built for a merchant and his family,
similar to the Gamulls' in Chester.

Montacute House, Somerset
(www.montacute@nationaltrust.org.uk)
This is a large Tudor mansion, similar to
Ingatestone Hall, Catherine's home.

Index

Acknowledgements

I would like to thank the following for their help and
support: James Turtle, Gloucestershire Record Office;
John Purkis; Pam Lynch, St Mary's Heritage Centre,
Chester; Janet Axworthy, Chester Education; Ruth
Gallagher, Chester College; Helen Holyoak, King's
School, Chester.

Photographs: Bodleian Library, Oxford; 5t, 18; Cheshire County
Council, Chester: 4b, 23; Essex Record Office: 8; Gloucestershire
Record Office: 4t, 5m, 5b, 12, 27; Guildhall Library, Corporation of
London: 29; Mary Evans Pictue Library: 21; Museum of London:
2, 28; Petre Family, Ingatestone Hall: 6; Sallie Purkis: 13; Weald &
Downland Open Air Museum: 16; t=top; m=middle; b=bottom.

Published 2004 by A&C Black Publishers Limited
37 Soho Square, London W1D 3QZ
www.acblack.com

ISBN 0-7136-6243-3

Copyright text © Sallie Purkis, 2004
Copyright illustrations © Anna C Leplar, 2004

A CIP record for this book is available from the British Library.

Printed in Singapore by Tien Wah Press (Pte) Ltd

A&C Black uses paper produced with elemental chlorine-free
pulp, harvested from managed sustainable forests.